A JUNIOR HISTORY

OF THE

AMERICAN NEGRO

Volume I

Discovery to the Civil War

Foreword by Kenneth B. Clark
City University of New York

A JUNIOR HISTORY
OF THE
AMERICAN NEGRO

Volume I

Discovery to the Civil War

by Morris C. Goodman

FLEET PRESS CORPORATION
NEW YORK and LONDON

For their assistance in providing illustrative material, the author expresses his thankfulness to the Schomburg Collection, the New York Public Library, and the Library of Congress.

Volume Two: THE CIVIL WAR TO THE CIVIL
RIGHTS WAR

© Copyright, 1969 Fleet Press Corporation
156 Fifth Avenue
New York City 10010

Library of Congress Catalogue Card No.: 73-76026

Manufactured in the United States of America

Dedicated to the children
I have taught and
their children

ABOUT THE AUTHOR

Dr. Morris C. Goodman is a native New Yorker and was educated at Columbia College, New York University, The New School, and Brooklyn College. He has taught for many years in the New York City schools and is presently senior editor of a New York publishing house. He is the author of several books and a contributor of numerous articles to national magazines.

Acknowledgments

This project was suggested by my publisher, Mrs. Doris Schiff, one of the very few women publishers in the United States. Her knowledge of my love for children and the understanding of their needs which I had acquired in a lifetime of teaching made her feel that it was one on which I would enjoy working. My thanks are due to her.

I am grateful to Mr. Gavin Thomson for his continuing interest in this work since its beginning, and for his wise counseling throughout its various stages.

Many friends in the New York City Board of Education have also read this work as it progressed and helped with their experienced eyes and professional comments. Among them are Mr. Allan Miller, Dr. James E. Devine, Mrs. Ellen M. Egan, and Mrs. Lenora Hahn. Miss Faye Simmons, of the Aguilar Branch, New York Public Library, has always been most cooperative, as have the members of the staff of the Schomburg Collection.

I am indebted to Dr. Kenneth B. Clark who took time from an extremely crowded schedule to read the book in manuscript and write the foreword.

Mr. Gonzalo Iglesias deserves thanks for his suggestions and help in preparing the manuscript for the press.

Foreword
by Kenneth B. Clark

Probably one of the most important educational respon-
sibilities facing America today is to build into the curriculum
at all levels sound and balanced accounts of the contribution
of ethnic groups to the vitality of America. The role of all
ethnic groups is neglected but probably the most neglected
is the Negro American. It is certainly quite possible to
contact graduates of American colleges and probably even
specialists in American history who believe that the growth
and development of America as a powerful industrial and
political nation does reflect primarily, if not exclusively, the
contributions of individuals of white and European origin.
Even the tortuous struggle to develop an effective democratic
base for the American political system is usually discussed and
taught chiefly in terms of contributions from Jefferson, Hamilton, Franklin and other founding fathers with respectable
Anglo-Saxon names.

This normal and accepted distortion of American history
has resulted in the educational deprivation of all American
children. Certainly it can be seen as an important factor in
the continuation of tensions and suspicions among the various
nationalities, religions and racial groups which comprise
America.

It has become increasingly clear that the role of education in neutralizing some of the more flagrant forms of racism has so far been minimal. It is now equally clear that education must play a foremost role in preparing American children to move critically and creatively within a world of diversity. Mutual respect and understanding of the contributions in common humanity of the various nationalities, of Negro Americans, and the various religions which make up America must now be central objectives of America. Morris C. Goodman's book *A Junior History of the American Negro* is an important contribution to the beginning of these approaches at the primary and secondary levels. It has established a sound basis for education at higher levels in this critical area.

City University of New York
February, 1969

Contents

INTRODUCTION

Land of the Free, or Home of the Slave?

When you watch birds in a birdbath in a garden, you see a strange sight. The same kind of birds bathe together while the other kinds wait their turn. All the black birds take a bath together. All the bluejays wait until the black birds finish. Then the bluejays take a bath. The sparrows and other little birds wait until the big birds finish. Then they take their bath.

People don't know why birds act like this. The birds can't talk to us and tell us why even if they know. But we do ask people why they act or behave the way they do. It is important to know because people with skins of different color must be able to get along together to make the world a better place to live in.

America has people of all colors. The red-skins or Indians lived here before the first white men came. The white men bought black men who were brought from Africa to do work for them. They were called slaves. This is a big idea to think about. The white men came here to be free, and then they enslaved men and women who were not freed until after a terrible conflict called the Civil War.

There are more grandchildren and great grandchildren of the black slaves now than there are red-skinned Indians or yellow-skinned people from the other side of the world. For a long time the black people were kept apart from the white people. They could not live together, bathe in the same pool, or sit in the same part of a movie theatre.

Laws to make everybody able to do the same things were passed. But there are places where blacks still have to fight for their rights. What they want is their "civil rights" to live, work, and enjoy life the same as white people.

A lot of people forget that the black people not only have the same rights as the white people, but that they helped make this country great. You are going to see how this happened and learn about the black people who helped build America.

Chapter I

The Beginnings of America

The Beginnings of America

In the 1600's in England, people had to be of the same religion as the King. It was the same in France. Things were made hard in these countries for anyone who believed in a different religion or worshipped God in a different way. It was so bad that they left to make a new home in the new country, America.

The Pilgrims came from England to be free, to show how they loved God in their own way—not the King's way. People came from France for the same reason. One father of a little French boy sent him all the way to America alone. He knew he would never see his boy again, but he wanted his son to grow up in a free country where he would not be hurt because he showed his love of God in a way that was different from the King's way.

The father arranged for the little boy to go to school in Boston to learn to read and write English, and then to learn to earn his money as a silversmith—a man who makes beautiful things of silver, like bowls, tea pots, knives, forks, and spoons. The little French boy went to the Boston Dame School where he had to pay a penny a day. All the teachers were women, and they soon found out that the little French boy was very bright. His name was Apollon Rivoire. He changed his name to make it easier for everybody to say. You have heard of him as Paul Revere.

Paul got good marks. When he finished school he became good at making things of silver. He made the first false teeth ever made in America—wooden ones for people who had lost their own teeth. He loved his new country, and when the King in far-away England made things hard for the people in the new colony, he did a lot to help make the people free from the Mother Country.

By this time, Paul was a man. To help show how things were in the fight between the Americans and the English, he drew pictures showing English soldiers killing Americans. One fight was so bad that it was called the Boston Massacre.

The death of Crispus Attucks in the Boston Massacre

In this picture you see Indians being killed by the British for helping the Americans who were fighting for freedom.

One of them was a great leader whose name was Crispus Attucks. But picture and history books didn't give credit to this brave man as a black leader; they said he was a Nantucket Indian. This was the beginning of ignoring the Negroes' part in American history.

From then on, and for a long time, black men and women received little or no credit for the great things they did for their own people and for all Americans. They were kept down by selfish people who only wanted them as slaves, not able to become free and equal in the land that was created where everybody could be free and equal.

"Window" view of a Slave Ship

From the days in the slave ships until today, the black man has put up a struggle to be free and equal, to get his rights. This is his story.

Chapter II

Getting the Color Picture in Focus

Getting the Color Picture in Focus

People of other colors tried to hide the good and the great things Negroes have done in the past. They hoped to keep the black people down by never giving them credit for helping to make history. But that isn't true. Even before Columbus came to America there was a strong land ruled by a super-king in Africa. It was the Songhay Empire. It had a college at Timbuctu where students from Africa, Asia, and Europe learned about great books. Some became doctors and lawyers there.

Many Negroes have given America wonderful help and proved that they can be leaders in war, in opening up new lands, in inventing new things, in being doctors, and in business. During the Revolution (or War for Independence), General George Washington had about 5,000 Negroes fighting against the British on the side of the colonies in both the army and the navy. In the War of 1812, when the English tried to get the new country back, there was a great battle at New Orleans, Louisiana. The American army there was led by General Andrew Jackson who had a great many black soldiers fighting side by side with him. That was the last time any other country tried to take over our country and rule here.

The Civil War was fought between the southern states and the northern states. One big reason for this war was slavery. The people of the South wanted to keep their black slaves. The people of the North wanted them to be free. President Lincoln said the slaves must be free. As President, what he said was law. To make the southern people obey the law and keep them from making the South a separate country or nation, he had to use soldiers. There were over 200,000 Negro soldiers who fought on the side of the North to keep our country together as one country. They helped to save our country as the *UNITED* (not separated) States, and to free the slaves.

After the Civil War, brave men started out to win the West. The land between the middle of America and the west coast was called the Wild West because it was really wild. Only Indians and a few Spanish explorers had ever been there. After the Civil War, the number of people grew. They needed more space, more land to live on, and more food. Lewis and Clark went west to explore this wild country. Fremont was also a leading explorer. These leaders and others took Negroes with them. In this way, many black men helped to win the West.

The Indians did not want the white men to take their land, their water and their hunting grounds away from them. They fought to keep what was theirs. The Indians didn't believe the white men would share what they had, and they tried to keep them out of the West. Geronimo and Sitting Bull were two of the Indian chiefs who tried to

A Negro Troop in the Civil War

hold on to their land for their people. The part they played in history has been shown many times in movies and on television. But the part played in history by the Negro soldiers has not been shown. The Negroes fought against the Apaches, the Sioux, and the Comanches. To help settle this wild land, armies were sent to patrol the newly won West. One out of every five soldiers doing the job of keeping the peace—from Canada to the Rio Grande River—and between St. Louis and the Rocky Mountains—was a Negro.

A Negro was one of the first men to reach the top of the world. He was Nat Henson who went with Peary to the North Pole in 1909. Black men were doing important things once they were freed. They invented helpful aids to man. A patent is an official government paper that protects an inventor from dishonest people who might try to use his invention without permission or payment. Hundreds and hundreds of patents were granted to Negroes after the Civil War, and their work helped make our country greater.

A Negro named Niño was with Columbus when he discovered America. Another was with Balboa when he discovered the Pacific Ocean. Arizona and New Mexico were territories opened by a Negro known as "Little Stevie," or Estevánico, in Spanish.

Two of our country's first women poets were Negroes, Lucy Terry and Phillis Wheatley. When our new Capitol, Washington, D.C., was planned and laid out, an assistant city planner on the job was a Negro named Benjamin Banneker.

James Beckwourth opened the Pass (short for passageway) named after him. Ira Aldridge was the star of an all-Negro theatre group that acted all over the world. Fourteen Negroes were elected to Congress after the Civil War.

So America became greater and greater in war and in peace through the help black men and women gave. They served in the army and navy, in making our country larger through winning the West, and in the fields of invention, science, the arts, and business.

Chapter III

>>>->>>->>>->>>->>>->>>->>>->>>->>>->>>· · ·<<<-<<<-<<<-<<<-<<<-<<<-<<<-<<<-<<<-<<<

Africa —
Homeland of the Black People

Africa —
Homeland of the Black People

The planet you live on is named "Earth." It is a small part of the solar system of heavenly bodies which has the sun at its center, making the seasons. The Earth is mainly covered by water. The biggest parts of land are called continents. There are seven continents. You live on the continent of North America.

Africa, where the slaves were taken from, is a very big continent. White men called this great land "the Dark Continent" or sometimes "Darkest Africa." The sun shines brighter on Africa than many other places, but it is still called dark. Why should this be? The answer is very important, but it is not easy nor simple.

The answer has to do with feelings, and with how words tell about feelings. If a boy is always smiling, we say he is "sunny" or "he has a sunny disposition." That word *sunny* comes from *sun* because when the sun is shining most people feel good.

The word *dark* gives the opposite kind of feeling. Most people are afraid of the dark. They don't know what there might be in the dark, and they are afraid of the mystery. People call things they don't know about *dark*. They call them a dark secret or a dark mystery.

In this way the word dark and the word black have a lot to do with how Africa and Africans have been treated by white men. The people of Africa had no alphabet, so the history of their countries had never been written. This made their past a dark mystery—something that made the white man feel more important because his history was written.

Then the people were dark. The white men thought they were not important because their color was not the same, and that they must be at least half wild, like animals. Even white priests and ministers had the idea that these strange dark people must be creatures that God put a curse on.

No one took the time to ask the black people of Africa questions like, "What do you know?" "Does your history go back far?" "What can you make, or grow, or paint, or sew, or carve?" The white man had no time for questions either. What he saw was a living thing worth money. He didn't understand the sounds they made, and so he put them in chains to sell as slaves.

History is a record of what happens to people. It is usually written down. But the African people told their history, and it was not lost, and some of it is known today. What we know shows that all of Africa was not wild, savage, or animal-like. The black people of Africa who were made slaves had grandparents who were capable in many ways.

A thousand years ago Ghana was a great nation in Africa. It was already a country a thousand years old. The people lived in peace. They were mostly farmers, but they had a

Slaves were still put in chains, just before the Civil War

great army of thousands of soldiers to protect them. Four to five hundred years ago, Ghana also was a business country. They sold ivory and gold, or exchanged them.

Ghana became a rich country. Its biggest town was Kumbi where business was done, where ivory could be exchanged for salt, or gold for cloth. It was a big center where dealers met for this exchange, where even slaves were sold in the market.

The head of this country was called the Tunka, a title like emperor or king. He lived in a beautiful palace with painted or colored windows, statues, and pictures. He wore a silk outfit with gold bracelets and other jewelry. He acted as a judge to his people, giving out punishments to the bad, and medals and prizes to the good.

White Christians were not the first to come to Ghana. The Islams, Arab people, who believed in Mohammed the way Christians believe in Christ, went to the land of Melle,

31

in the year 1076. There they killed the black people who would not believe in Mohammed. The others were allowed to live, and they became rich growing food, weaving cloth, making objects of clay, silver and gold, and putting up buildings.

The Mohammedans believe that to go to heaven when they die, they must first visit the City of Mecca. This trip is called a pilgrimage. Less than 300 years after the Mohammedans went to Melle, the King of Melle, who had become a Mohammedan, made the pilgrimage. In 1324 he went to Mecca with 60,000 of the people he ruled. Camels carried tons of gold, some of which the King gave to his people on the way as presents, the rest to be used to build houses of worship which are called "mosques" in the Mohammedan religion.

Songhay was a country of West Africa once ruled over by Melle. It became free and independent, and grew to be a rich land and the strongest in West Africa. The King of Songhay also made a pilgrimage to Mecca to learn how to make his nation greater through laws, schools, and business. This happened in 1497, only five years after Columbus discovered America.

All this shows that Africa was not all *DARK,* or "in the dark." The black people were studying at centers in Gao, Jenne, Timbuktu, and Walata. There were wise rulers, and the people learned how to live a good life, with families holding them together. They carved statues, and made beautiful objects of clay, copper, brass, gold and silver. They believed in their own gods.

There was one thing that held back the writing on stones and of history books. There were no alphabets, but there were over four hundred different languages or dialects—the spoken language of a small number of people in a tribe or clan. This also made the white man feel greater than the black man whose land had no written history, no printed Bible, and no real religion. So remember, Africa was not all dark before the white man came. Its history became much darker after.

Chapter IV

﹥﹥﹥﹥﹥﹥﹥﹥﹥﹥﹥﹥﹥﹥﹥ · ﹤﹤﹤﹤﹤﹤﹤﹤﹤﹤﹤﹤﹤﹤﹤﹤

Discovery to Revolution
1492 - 1776

Discovery to Revolution
1492 - 1776

When people need things, or they can get a lot of money for them, they will go anywhere to look for them. There were no ice boxes or refrigerators 500 years ago. There was no dry cleaner where a lady could have her dresses cleaned. Because there was no way to keep meat fresh, people used pepper and other spices to make it taste better. Rich ladies needed perfumes to take away the smell of clothes that were never cleaned.

These are only two of the things people wanted and had to get from far away lands. Brave men tried to find new ways to get from Europe to India to get some of the things that were wanted and that they could get a lot of money for. The old way they knew to get to India took a long, long time. They were looking for a short cut.

Christopher Columbus was not looking for a new land when he discovered America. He was trying to find a short way to India. He landed on this side of the Atlantic Ocean, and he thought it was India. That is how the red-skinned people Columbus found here got their name. Columbus thought he was in India, that the people were Indians.

In the 1400's and 1500's, men looking for a short cut to India got into parts of Africa. They took Africans back to Europe with them. Then, when they tried again to find the short way to India, they took Africans to the New World, afterwards named America, after the explorer, Amerigo Vespucci.

The European countries of Spain and Portugal were rich and powerful in those days. They sent their explorers to find a new way to India, or paid their expenses if they came from a different country. Columbus was an Italian, but the King and Queen of Spain gave him the men, money, and ships to find a new way to India. It was by accident that he found the New World. But it was no accident that he had Negroes with him on the ocean voyage. It was with these black men who sailed with Columbus that the history of the Negro in America begins. Other explorers like Cortez, De Soto, de Vaca, Joliet, Marquette, and Pizarro brought Negroes with them to the New World after Columbus.

The explorers tried to build a new nation for their kings and queens in the New World. Being far from the "mother country," the new lands were called colonies.

Lucas Vasquez de Allyón, a Spaniard, brought the first Africans to settle in the New World. In the summer of 1526 he cleared land in what is now South Carolina, at the mouth of the Pee Dee River.

The colony failed. Many Spaniards got sick and died. The leaders fought with each other. Even with four Spaniards to each Negro, the whites lost control of the Africans. When winter came the black men fought the whites and won. The Spaniards still alive sailed away to Haiti. The Negroes who remained behind joined up with the Indians. It was the end of the colony, but it was the beginning of a new life for the black people in a place that became a part of the United States.

In other parts of the New World Negroes helped open up new lands. When Columbus discovered America, a Negro named Pedro Alonso Niño was with him. Except for the Indians, the first eyes to see the Pacific Ocean were those of a white man and a black man. When the Portuguese Balboa discovered this great body of water, the Negro Nunno de Olando was with him. A dozen years after the Pee Dee colony broke up, an African, Estevánico, meaning Little Stephen or Stevie, went exploring for gold with Cabeza de Vaca. It was on a treasure hunt that this Negro opened up the new lands of Arizona and New Mexico in 1538. It was Estevánico who was the leader, at the head of the Spanish men.

Estevánico originally came from the western coast of Morocco. He was a slave owned by a Spaniard, and became one of a party of four hundred men aiming to explore Florida. In 1528, they arrived in the New World near the Bay of Tampa, Florida. Only four of the four hundred lived; all the rest were lost. The four who survived were Estevánico, his owner, and two others.

The four were marooned on the coast of Texas where they were captured and made slaves by the Indians. It took them seven years to free themselves. They traveled all across Texas and Mexico to the territory called New Spain. When they told all they had seen, their story became the starting point of the Coronado Expedition. Estevánico went on exploring. He was the discoverer of the New Mexico Pueblos. Death came to this Negro explorer in 1839 at the hands of the Zuñi Indians in the territory.

The Spaniards and Portuguese in the New World made slaves of the Indians, but this did not work out. The Indian was on his home base, and he put up a terrible fight. The Indian knew his land and could escape from slavery back to his own tribe where the white man couldn't find him. The different way of life was hard on many Indians who died as slaves, or died of white man's diseases.

The way is worked out, the problem was solved by having slaves do the work. The first black people brought to the part of the New World under the rule of the English King arrived at Jamestown, Virginia in 1619. They were not brought as slaves, but as indentured servants—people who came to work for a certain number of years to pay for their fare and their keep, and then became free.

This did not last long. The black people were badly needed for work, and by 1661 all Negroes coming to Virginia from Africa were made slaves forever by law. If they had children born in Virginia, the law said the children were also to be slaves forever.

The black man was a much bigger help to the white man than the Indian. The African knew how to farm from home. He was too far from home ever to get back. He could be caught because of his color if he ran away.

For a hundred years after the first Negroes were brought to America, the slave trade grew bigger and bigger. They were sold to tobacco planters in Maryland, Virginia and South Carolina. They were bought by growers of rice in Georgia and South Carolina. In less than 100 years after the first ship load arrived at Jamestown, these five colonies had 35,000 slaves.

Because the middle colonies like New York, New Jersey, Delaware, and Pennsylvania were bigger in business than planting, not as many slaves were used there. There were probably little more than 10,000 compared to the 35,000 in the southern colonies at the same time. Farthest north, there were about 2,000 slaves.

Wherever there was a use for them in the colonies, there were slaves. There were more and more slaves as time passed, until one out of every five people in the colonies was a slave. They worked on farms, in the army, in factories, on fishing boats, and in homes.

Today we take polls to find out what people think about a man running for president, or about a war, or any big public question. What was the opinion of people on slavery during colonial times?

The slaves were against it, of course. They began to show it on the ships bringing them from Africa; 150 revolts took place on the slave ships. In New York City, in 1712, about thirty slaves and Indians killed and wounded about fifteen white men with guns and knives. Seventy slaves were put in prison; the ones found guilty were hanged or burned alive.

In 1741, another riot took place in New York. It was a bad winter, and both slaves and poor whites had a hard time. There was looting, and fires were set. Over one hundred and fifty Negroes and twenty-five poor whites were arrested, and many of them were killed.

The slave owners were for slavery. They had the law on their side—the Black Code, as it was called. The laws stated what a black man could and could not do. A slave could work sixteen hours a day, could meet together with only a couple of other slaves, could own no guns or any rum or whisky, and could be beaten to death by his owner if he had to be punished.

Not only the slaves were against slavery. Many white

people were against it and wanted it stopped at once. Some people saw it as coming to an end a little at a time, gradually, as the Negroes learned more. In 1688, the Quakers of Pennsylvania made a protest against slavery. George Washington said it was trouble to own slaves.

Negroes in the western hemisphere were making some progress and some real friends. The priests in the Catholic colonies in Latin America tried to protect the slaves and to get their owners to free them. Brother Martin in Peru was one of the first Negroes to become a priest, and was made a saint in 1962.

Two freed slaves who became famous as poets, Lucy Terry and Phillis Wheatley, visited George Washington.

The true story of Lucy Terry is like one in a book. She advanced from being a slave girl to being a leader of the black people. Her fame began one day when there was an Indian raid on the village where she lived, Deerfield, Massachusetts. It took place August 25, 1746. This girl, the property of Ensign Wells, saw the bloody killings, and although she never went to any school, she was educated enough in English to write a poem about all she saw. Experts say that the poem, "Bars Fight," gives the true story of what happened on that awful day.

Lucy married a free Negro and became Mrs. Prince. People loved to come and listen to her tell stories. She spoke with great power. Once she used her gift of speech to try to get her son into a white college. Another time, she spoke right to the Justices of the Supreme Court when she felt the lawyer she had was not doing his job right. A man was trying to take some land away from her; she sued and the case went to the Supreme Court where the Justices said she spoke as well as many a lawyer. Lucy was honored for her fight for freedom of the slaves and for her wonderful poems, being proclaimed as the first Negro writer of poetry in America.

In 1761, Mrs. Susannah Wheatley, the wife of a Boston tailor, was so attracted to a little girl for sale in the slave market that she bought her at once, and took her home where she became almost a member of the family. Mrs.

Phillis Wheatley

Wheatley gave the girl the name Phillis; her daughter helped her to learn to read and write, for there was no law in Massachusetts against a Negro's learning as there was in other colonies. Phillis helped around the house, but spent most of her time in learning; soon she was as good at Latin as English, and wrote translations from Latin that were printed in the Old World and the New. Then she began to write poems.

While on a visit to England with Mrs. Wheatley's son, Phillis met many aristocrats, and a book of her poems was published there. She was entertained by the finest families, and would have met the King, too, if she did not feel the need to return to Boston because Mrs. Wheatley was ill. Her poems were printed in a book in America, and her fame spread. She made an unfortunate marriage to a man who did not appreciate her and was jealous. Her life changed. She had to work as a servant to support her husband and children, but she did compose a poem to George Washington. He felt greatly honored, and she visited him.

Her poems express her gentle nature, and her hopes for her people. Her life is an expression of belief in God and the good that would eventually come to all the Negro people.

These are only examples of a few of the Negroes who got ahead in life. Other freed slaves became rich and famous as doctors, cooks, bakers, and teachers.

Not all the colonial world thought "black" and "white."

Many great colonial leaders, like William Penn, the Quaker, George Washington, the Father of our Country, Tom Paine, the writer, Benjamin Franklin, the diplomat, and Patrick Henry, the great patriot, hoped for the day when all slaves would be free in the land where the idea of democracy was born.

Chapter V

·····

The Revolution
1776 - 1815

The Revolution
1776 - 1815

PART I

There were thirteen English colonies in the New World.
Each had a governor appointed by the King who was the
real ruler in the Mother Country. The people in the colonies
had a list of unfair taxes and duties. They wanted to rule
themselves. All this was written down in the Declaration of
Independence, and the thirteen colonies broke away from
the Mother Country.

War broke out. England wanted to keep the colonies. The
colonies wanted to be free. The King's soldiers fought the
American colonists, who were English and people of mixed
nations, under their leader, George Washington. Negroes
fought on both sides, the King's side and the colonists' side.
History books call the war both the Revolution and the War
for Independence. It started in 1776.

Before the actual Declaration of Independence was signed
by the leaders of the colonists, small fights or skirmishes
between the English and Americans had taken place. One
of these was the Boston Massacre which took place in 1770,

in which the runaway slave, Crispus Attucks, was killed. His story is told at the beginning of this book. The war ended in 1781, when the British under General Cornwallis surrendered at Yorktown. Between these two dates, five thousand Negroes fought on the side of the American colonists. They did their part for victory with the Minute Men at Lexington and Concord. Negroes were with General Washington at the Battle of Valley Forge, and when he crossed the Delaware. There were Negro pilots who guided ships in the colonial navy under the command of John Paul Jones, and others who were spies for the colonists.

The English thought it was a good idea to have Negroes on their side. One English Governor, Lord Dunmore of Virginia, schemed to get the unhappy slaves on his side by freeing them if they would fight for the King. Sometimes he forced freedom on the slaves to make English soldiers of them. His activities ended when the colonists defeated him at Great Bridge. But his scheme kept working, and thousands of Negroes became free by serving the British as soldiers, spies, workmen, and guides. When the war was over, and soldiers in the King's army and sailors in the King's navy were leaving their stations and their ships, hundreds of Negroes were found among them in places like Charleston, Savannah, and New York.

Until the war broke out, no Negro was allowed to handle a gun or anything, including tools, that had the power to kill. These laws were called Black Codes. But when both sides wanted the help of Negroes, both sides made fighters of them.

A fighting man does his best when he loves what he is fighting for. The slaves loved the ideas in the Declaration of Independence which said all men have the right to life, liberty, and the pursuit of happiness. This paper held out a promise of human brotherhood, of equality, and of liberty. That is why they fought well, why they were praised by their generals as being best dressed, best in manners, and best in battle. The Negroes knew what they were fighting for, and so they fought with pride. There was not a battle in the Revolution to which they did not add their ability and their bravery.

The wonderful new ideas in the Declaration of Independence about freedom, liberty, brotherhood, happiness and rights made more and more people believe that slavery was evil. The American colonists fought to be free from English rule; why shouldn't the slaves be free? To do away with anything is to abolish it; the word *abolition* comes from this, and was given to big clubs or societies whose aim was the abolition of slavery. In New York, Alexander Hamilton, who signed the Declaration and became the new country's first Secretary of the Treasury, formed an abolitionist society. In Philadelphia, Benjamin Franklin, another signer and future

Benjamin Franklin

ambassador to France, did the same. People were accepting freedom, and in many places slavery was abolished. Franklin was the first president of his society. To show the aims of the people who thought the same as he did, he named it "The Pennsylvania Society for Promoting the Abolition of Slavery and the Relief of Free Negroes unlawfully held in Bondage."

PART II

The Declaration of Independence which declared all men "free and equal" did not free the slaves. While Penn and Franklin and many more fought hard to free the slaves, other people had different ideas.

The slave owners themselves did not, of course, want to give up the slaves and lose the money they had paid for them, or the work the slaves did for them.

Let us look at some of the other ways different people thought about the slaves, and how different kinds of action followed different ways of thinking. This will show you again that ideas are not always all "black" or all "white." Do you remember what Lord Dunmore did in Virginia? He freed any slave who would fight for the King. After the Revolution, the men who made the laws in New Jersey freed the slaves of any owner who had been on the King's side.

The man whose job was to get the money for the colonists to pay for the war, Robert Morris, thought the slaves should be freed little by little. He hoped this would work out better than quick and total abolition.

Thomas Jefferson, who helped write the Constitution of the new nation, believed in God, blamed the King of England for slavery, and thought the white man was superior to the Negro. In the way he helped write the Constitution, he still tried to keep the slave owners on his side.

The Marquis de Lafayette who came to America from France to help the colonists win freedom became a great friend of George Washington. He asked Washington to buy land where slaves could be tenants, working as free people, and paying rent. The idea came to nothing.

Another soldier who came from Europe to help in the Revolution was General Thaddeus Kosciusko from Poland. His idea was to educate all the slaves, and he gave all his money for this cause.

In 1781 the war was over. The new nation had to have a way of working. A plan had to be made and put in writing; it would become the highest law in the land, and would be called the Constitution of the United States of America.

Thomas Jefferson is called the Father of the Constitution. He is given credit for writing most of it. Before any part of this great plan of how the new nation was to work was written down, it was proposed, discussed, and very often fought over. One of the biggest fights was over slavery.

The slave-owners wanted to have the slaves counted towards how many representatives or congressmen each new state would have. This would give more votes in Congress to slave states than to free states. The slave states would get credit for having people who could not vote, who were in a place they were brought to against their will, and who did not want to be there! The anti-slavery leaders were horrified by this, but were afraid the Union of the colonies would be broken into pieces. To keep all thirteen colonies together, each side gave in a little, and they finally decided:

1. To count slaves as three-fifths of other persons. This became known as "the three-fifths compromise."
2. To let the slave trade go on for another 20 years, ending in 1808.
3. To make it a duty of the finder to return any fugitive runaway slave to his owner.

This was a terrible setback for the freedom movement. One man, George Mason, who helped Jefferson with the Constitution, called it a "national sin," which, he said would be followed by "national calamities."

Where were the victims of this terrible setback, the Negroes, during this period of time? Most were doing slave labor on the plantations. Some were freed, and went on to give great help to the new nation and to their own people. Many fought bravely against the English who tried to get back their old "colonies," which had become the United States of America.

The most famous Negro of his time was Benjamin Banneker—a genius who mastered two of the hardest subjects: mathematics and astronomy (the science of the stars). He did this although he had almost no schooling. Born in Ellicott, Maryland, on November 9, 1731, Benjamin became famous in his early youth. He made a wooden clock while he was still quite young. It may have been the first clock ever made in America, and it still kept time after he died.

During the 75 years of his life he was known for all he did in science, mathematics, and astronomy, for his writings on these subjects and on the subject of freeing the slaves. For some time he ran a farm. He sold it to give more time to study and writing. It seemed there was no mathematics problem he could not solve.

Many people who heard about Benjamin's brilliance and his strange way of living went to see him. They were curious about the clever man who could solve all mathematics problems, and who liked to stay awake all night to gaze at the stars. He was polite to all his visitors, showing them everything about the place he lived.

His star-gazing was not just an idle waste of time; it led to great knowledge of the movement of the planets, the position of the stars, and the phases of the moon. This knowledge led him in 1792 to start publishing an Almanac containing this information which is of use in telling the weather ahead of time, help in farming and sailing, and understanding the seasons. Banneker published the Almanac every year until 1806.

He felt very strongly about slavery and wrote letters to great men about it, asking for their help in ending it. His writing also appeared in little booklets or pamphlets for the general public to read. Thomas Jefferson was very much impressed by Banneker's work in science and in his efforts to bring an end to slavery. Jefferson sent Banneker's writings on science to the leading scientists of France, who read with great respect this brilliant Negro's work. Jefferson also succeeded in getting George Washington to appoint Banneker to help plan the new capitol of the nation, Washington, District of Columbia.

Benjamin Banneker is an example of what a free man can accomplish, no matter what his color. No slave could have achieved what Benjamin Banneker did.

Other Negroes were outstanding.

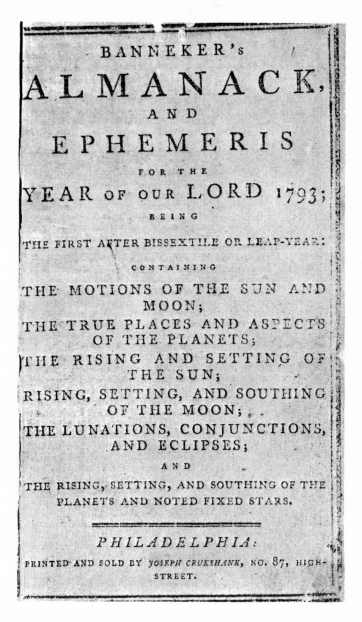

BANNEKER's

ALMANACK,

AND

EPHEMERIS

FOR THE

YEAR OF OUR LORD 1793;

BEING

THE FIRST AFTER BISSEXTILE OR LEAP-YEAR:

CONTAINING

THE MOTIONS OF THE SUN AND MOON;

THE TRUE PLACES AND ASPECTS OF THE PLANETS;

THE RISING AND SETTING OF THE SUN;

RISING, SETTING, AND SOUTHING OF THE MOON;

THE LUNATIONS, CONJUNCTIONS, AND ECLIPSES;

AND

THE RISING, SETTING, AND SOUTHING OF THE PLANETS AND NOTED FIXED STARS.

PHILADELPHIA:

PRINTED AND SOLD BY *JOSEPH CRUKSHANK*, NO. 87, HIGH-STREET.

The title page of Banneker's "Alamanack" for the year 1793

Because they were put out of a white people's church in Philadelphia, two Negroes, Richard Allen and Absolom Jones,

The Reverend Richard Allen   The Reverend Absalom Jones

formed their own church for the black people. They called this first house of prayer for Negroes the African Methodist Episcopal Church, and Richard Allen became its first bishop.

Negroes fought in the navy against the British in the War of 1812. One out of every six men in the American navy was a Negro, and all were praised for their bravery. They also volunteered in the army, winning the praise of General Andrew Jackson who gave a Negro credit for firing the shot that killed General Packenham of the English army.

During this period, everything in the new nation was growing. The amount of cotton produced grew. The number of white people grew. The number of black people grew. And the need for more space, for more land, grew. There was only one place to go. West!

Chapter VI

The Movement West

The Movement West

Just as we have repeated that nothing is really all black or all white, we must remember that what this means to you who are studying history is that there may be more than two sides to any story.

The dark side of the story of the Constitutional Convention was the setback to the cause of abolition. The bright side of the history of that year, 1787, was the passing of the Northwest Ordinance, a law against slavery in all land north of the Ohio River.

While the slavery question got no real answer, the problem of more space was being solved by the movement to the West. The pioneers were people of every race, color and religion who went west looking for a place to live and build homes. Some Negroes went to trap animals for the fur trade or as guides because the Indians trusted them; others went to dig for gold in the mines.

When Lewis and Clark started out on their expedition west, at least one Negro is known to have gone with them.

This was the first expedition officially started by the United States government. Its purpose was to learn more about the continent of North America. William Clark had a slave whose name was York. He stayed with Clark from the

The Lewis and Clark Expedition while on the Columbia River

beginning of the journey in 1804 until the end in 1806. They started out near the beginning of the Missouri River, in a sailing boat, crossed the Rocky Mountains and the Bitterroot Mountains, and traveled to the Columbia River's mouth.

John C. Fremont made four expeditions to open the Northwest lands. Jacob Dodson, a free Negro, went with Fremont on his journey to find a new pass through the High Sierra in 1843. Saunders Jackson, another free Negro, went with Fremont in 1848 on his fourth expedition.

The Negroes who joined the westward movement were of all kinds. Some went as slaves with their masters. Some took off as runaway slaves. Some were actually free men and women. They took part in the movement west. Some went all the way from the swamps of Florida to the coast of California. There were Negroes who took part, as time went on, in the rush for gold to California. There were Negroes along when the Mormons had to move further and further west as they were pushed out of other settlements because their religion permitted a man to have as many wives as he wanted.

As Florida was still a colony belonging to Spain, it was a wonderful hiding place for runaway slaves. The Indians in Florida and the Negroes shared something: the white enemy. Besides, the swamps were a perfect place to remain out of the white man's sight.

Florida was not only a safe place for runaway slaves, it was also a place where they were welcome. The Negroes who were able to cross the border joined up with the Seminole Tribe. No count could be kept, but it is likely that thousands got away, built homes, farmed, and bred livestock, horses, and cattle.

The slave owners naturally wanted the United States government to get their living, human property returned to them. They wanted revenge on the Indians who helped the slaves. They made such an angry noise about losing their slaves that the United States government made war on the Seminoles three times. They had a good basis for their claim. The first American Treaty of 1790 said that Indians must return runaway slaves. Money was spent, blood was spilled, lives were lost. In the end, after the third and last of these wars (which lasted eight years) some Indians and some

Negroes joined the westward movement; they pushed on to Oklahoma. By 1816, American soldiers were attacking a Negro fort in Florida under federal government orders.

Some Negroes became members of Indian tribes. One, James Beckwourth, even became an Indian Chief, head of the Crow Tribe. He helped the Crows win many victories over their enemies, and was buried in their own cemetery so his spirit would always be with his adopted people.

Long before the Negro's hands were free to work for himself, he was busy branding and tying up cattle. There were many black cowboys although you don't see many of them as heroes of western movies. Few people remember them today, but there was a time when the trails were filled with Negro cowboys and the millions of cattle that they moved on the long drive west.

There was real equality among the black, brown, red, and white cowboys as the riders of the trails were Negroes, Mexicans, Indians and white westerners. They had the same daily life of thrills and danger out in the open under the sky. While they shared storms and stampedes, gunfire and floods, at the end of the trail there was no place for the Negroes in the corral. They didn't have to sing, "Don't Fence Me In"; they were never let inside. But even if they were a breed of vanishing Americans (second after the Indians), they still did a fabulous job in helping to build the West, and they were a part of that great adventure—one part, but at least an equal part, and maybe a larger one when it comes to counting them.

Negro soldiers did a great deal to help open the West. They were brave and reliable. Their heroism against Indians who attacked white settlements was a big feature in making it possible to settle in new lands. For over twenty years before the Civil War, and for a long time after, Texan Negroes helped against Indian attacks. Along with the coming of the Texan ranchers and cattlemen were the Negro cowboys.

The white and Negro cowboys lived the same kind of life. They rode the trails. They whooped it up in the streets of the cowtowns when the job was done. In the larger cities, they walked around, often getting into fights and using guns, pistols, and even their bullwhips. They took dangerous chances, going through outlaw land carrying precious gold. Often they got into fights between ranchers and cattlemen over land. All in all, the cowboys were alike in their way of life, in the danger they shared, the fun they had, and the part they played in the winning of the West. Only when the West was won, the Negro cowboys were not welcome to remain, nor did history make them the heroes they really were.

The Negro cowboys should not be forgotten because they put their brand on the history of the westward movement. Some of the new ranchers of the West brought slaves with them from their homes in the South. In the new land, the slaves learned from the Mexican, Indian and white cowboys.

The movies have shown the trek to the West in hundreds of "westerns." Until 1967, when Sammy Davis, Jr. played a cowboy role in a movie, no other Negro cowboy had ever been shown. Yet that trek west was made by Negroes from the time of exploration until the slaves were taken along in the movement westward.

The Negroes moved west in covered wagons; some wlked, driving cattle, pigs, and oxen before them. Death came from bad weather, drownings, and accidents. Often the Negro slaves were protected by their owners by being kept from the more dangerous jobs the cowboys had to do. Bronco busting, or breaking a wild horse, was done more often by white cowboys than by the blacks. This was because the white masters were afraid the slaves might be hurt or killed, and the slaves were more valuable in cash than the whites working on the job. Often a slave might be worth as much as a thousand dollars, a great deal of money in those days.

Eastern Texas had a large number of Negro cowboys. Some ranches had crews made up only of Negroes. Before the Civil War, a number of free Negroes ran cattle in this part of Texas. One, Aaron Ashworth, had a larger herd of cattle than any other rancher—over 2,500 head. He himself was a slave owner, and he had a white teacher for his children. Ashworth was so well liked that he was allowed to remain in Texas (then a separate nation, not a part of the United States) after all the free Negroes were ordered out. A special law was passed by the Texas Congress to allow him to remain; later, another law allowed other free Negroes to stay there, too.

In the Indian nations, north of Texas, there were thousands of Negroes, some free, some slaves. The slaves belonged to Indians in the Five Tribes: the Cherokees, Chicksaws, Chocktaws, Creeks, and Seminoles; these were known as the civilized tribes. The slaves did farm work, or the work of cowboys. Texas and the Indian nations were the scenes of the beginning of the story of the Negro cowboy.

More and more slaves were bought by Texans. They were freed by the Civil War, and those best prepared to earn a living were the black cowboys. While there was strong feeling against the blacks in Texas for a long time after the Civil War, the cowboys were really better off than other Negroes. They had a place in the working set-up and in the social life. On a ranch every man had a post, like in the army. He could be promoted, although he could not get as high as being foreman. But the Negro and white cowboys, although it was rough, did live, eat, and work together.

There were so many cows and bulls on the loose after the Civil War, because there was no one to tend them during it, that the big job of the cowboys was to round them up. The cowboys went after these animals which had turned wild in the brush and coulees (or valleys). They rode out with hardly anything but their small supply of food, their corn bread, dried meat, and, of course, their rope to lasso the animals.

One of these hunters was known as the Coyote. He was a Negro cowboy whose real name was Henry Beckwith. Henry got the name of Coyote because he was so much like that prairie wolf which needs hardly any sleep. He was as tough and untamed as that wild animal that the Shoshone Indians gave the name *coyotl*. Beckwith seemed to hunt with his ears and nose more than with his eyes because it was so hard to see in those places thick with shrubs where the animals went into hiding. Henry did not even carry bedding, but slept on the ground or used his horse's blanket. He could take a nap, drink a powerful mixture of black coffee and chili sauce, and start right out riding again. That is what the black cowboys of those days were like!

Texas was not yet a part of the United States, but a part of Mexico. A tough man ruled Mexico. His name was Antonio López de Santa Anna. The new Texans wanted to be free, to have their own country and rule themselves. The Texans fought against Santa Anna, and the Negroes fought beside them. Negroes were with the Texans when they lost the famous Battle of the Alamo, and they were with them when they won the war in the Battle of San Jacinto. The Negroes' help in fighting for the freedom of Texas was very soon forgotten, and they lost their own. The Texans took their freedom away and only wanted them out of the Republic they had helped to create.

When the westward march reached California, the Negro slaves helped their owners in the gold mines. Some were set free for the help they gave or the luck they struck. Many became rich themselves, or held good jobs as civil servants working for the government as teachers, or in other jobs as miners, express riders, and even as land owners. Even before the Civil War, in the 1850's, many of them held meetings to demand their civil rights, which was a small beginning of the whole Civil Rights Movement.

Although the Negroes helped open the West and build it, they were not really wanted in that part of the country. As usual there were two sides to the question: should the new states in the West be free states or slave states? It was a battle between the slave owners and the abolitionists all over again. Some of these fights were more than a war of words. Real battles broke out. The westerners wanted freedom for the slaves, but not on *their* land.

And still Negroes did a great deal to help in the building of the West. William Leidesdorf, a Negro, got to California in 1841, when it still belonged to Spain. He became one of its richest citizens and a great leader in government affairs. In 1844, George W. Bush did the pioneer job of leading the white people into the land which became Oregon. Before his death, Beckwourth, the adopted Crow Chief, opened a passage through the Sierra Nevada Mountains in 1850. It was named after this runaway slave, and appears on the map today as *Beckwourth Pass.*

Somehow, the score never seemed to even itself. The Negroes helped to open the West, and then the white men

James Beckwourth, adopted Crow Chief and
discoverer of the pass named after him

closed it to them. The West, where black men were not wanted, was against slavery. In the South, where the slave trade was permitted by law, it was to end in 1808. There slavery was wanted, and the number of slaves grew and grew! When the Revolution ended, there were fewer than a half million slaves in the New World. When the Civil War ended, there were four million Negroes in the United States. What was happening in the South?

Chapter VII

The Years of Slavery in the South

The Years of Slavery in the South

"First conquer, then enslave." These words were the slogan of generals, commanders, army chiefs, explorers, discoverers, and adventurers from olden times. These words mean that when a stronger force takes over a weaker one, the winner makes slaves of the losers. History is full of examples of this from the days when the Romans enslaved the Greeks right up to the time of Adolph Hitler.

When the Spaniards and the Portuguese came to the New World in the 1400's, they took the land belonging to the Indians and then made slaves of them. But it didn't work. The Indians were hunters, and what the white men needed was farmers. The Indians were a free people, and the hard work of a slave was actually enough to kill them. Their bodies could not fight the sicknesses they caught from their white masters, and this was another cause of death among them. Then, if they ran away, they were able to stay hidden in a land they knew much better than their masters.

But the Spaniards and Portuguese needed workmen and

planters, so they turned to the continent where they could get people who were used to staying in one place and farming: Africa. This was the beginning of the terrible African slave trade, the buying and selling of human beings, the capture of free souls and taking them thousands of miles from their homes and loved ones.

By the time the westward movement began the number of people in the southern states had become extremely large. As cotton became more important, the southern plantations needed more and more slaves. The number of southerners was growing so fast that by the time the Civil War started, there were eight million whites to four million Negroes, 2 to 1 of each color. Not all whites owned slaves; not all blacks were slaves. There were roughly a quarter of a million slave owners, and a quarter of a million free blacks.

Who were the slave owners? There was no one kind of slave owner. Most owners had only one slave, or just a few slaves. But one out of every ten slave owners (in the South) had 50 or more slaves. These were the tough-minded, hard-hearted ones who wanted to hold their living, human property. They didn't want anything "down South" that would spread ideas about being free or about being equal. For this reason they were against education, liberty, progress, democracy, voting (except by the rich), books, entertainment—anything that might give the Negroes the idea that they were as good as the whites. The slave owners promoted the idea, instead, of white supremacy. They believed God had made the white man (even the poor one) better than the Negro.

The slave owner was willing to make up any lie that enabled him to hold on to his rice, tobacco, sugar, and cotton plantation. He wished to spend his time without having to work, to have the power of money, even the power over life itself. All this depended on having slaves.

What was it like to be a slave? In the master's home on a big plantation, life was a little easier for the slaves who worked there. They were the "house negroes" and served as cooks, bakers, butlers, chambermaids, gardeners, coachmen, and often as nurses to the white babies or growing children. The women slaves were the "mammies"; the men slaves were the bodyguards. They were loosely members of the family, sharing the master's sadnesses and his celebrations. Many owners grew fond of them and talked about them as though they were overgrown children.

But in this situation the slaves were still slaves. They never went to school. They were not allowed to enjoy most activities of the whites. They lived or existed without the hope of ever becoming free. Yet, it was a good life compared to the life of the workers in the fields who produced cotton, rice, tobacco, and sugar with their back-breaking labor, sweat, and pain. By day they worked in the fields from the time the sun rose until it set during the season for planting, tending crops, and then picking or harvesting them.

The work in the fields was done under a gang boss called a "driver", from which we get the word slave-driver, still used today. In the off-season, during the winter months, the slaves pulled up trees, stumps, and bushes to have new land cleared for more planting; they put up or repaired fences; helped improve the water supply by digging ditches.

There were slaves in the cities of the South, too. Theirs was a different life, a little better life. The "driver" did not play a part in this. The skills or abilities of the city-slaves often made it possible for them to bargain and make agreements, even for getting pay for overtime work in a small degree. Their work was not simple plantation labor, but building, or working as waiters and maids, running machines in factories, and even doing work in science laboratories.

The free Negroes in the cities tried to make a better life for themselves and help the slaves. Many did all they could to help runaway slaves get to free states, to the North, and to Canada. Some bought their friends and relatives from their white masters. They became slave owners themselves in this way, because the Negroes they bought could not be freed but could lead a better life under their black owners. One free Negro invented a machine that changed the whole process of refining sugar all over the world. He was Norbert Rillieux, born in New Orleans. His fame reached all over the world because of this vacuum cup that was recognized as

Norman Rillieux whose invention changed the sugar business

71

a great accomplishment. A tablet was put on the wall of the Louisiana State Museum in 1934 telling of Rillieux's fame.

Life did not stand still during the time of slavery in the South. The evils of the Black Codes or the Slave Codes still made it illegal (against the law) for slaves to go to school, to meet in groups, to own guns, or even to protect themselves. But things were happening and changing all the time.

"Necessity is the mother of invention." This old saying tells us that when man has some great need, someone will invent a way to fill it. A faster way of producing cotton was badly needed. This need was filled by the invention of the cotton gin by Eli Whitney, a northerner, in 1793. This

The cotton gin at work

72

machine separates cotton fiber from the seeds, a labor that used to be done very slowly by hand. It is made of a cylinder with teeth that turns in circles around a grate with the raw cotton inside. The teeth catch the lint, pull it from the seeds, and the lint is removed from the cylinder by a revolving or turning brush.

This was the first of many changes in the South. The cotton gin was an invention that became the mother of necessity. It made growing more cotton necessary, and more and more slaves to plant it necessary. So, another change was the growth of slavery.

A newspaper cartoon showing a slave bearing
the burden of "King Cotton"

Cotton became the most important single product of the South. The cotton growers sold to the manufacturers of the North, England, and France. New machinery invented in England, which could spin fine thread to make cloth made the demand for raw cotton greater and greater. In the 50 years between 1810 and 1860 when the Civil War started, the cotton sent out by southern planters became worth 125 times more than it had been. It kept the mills and factories going, and it made the slave trade grow bigger aand bigger.

As the number of slaves grew larger, many made a try for freedom, and the pro-slavers made greater efforts to hold them down. Night watchers with vicious dogs roamed about to keep slaves from running away or meeting in groups to plot against their white masters.

Hopes of freedom never died, however, even though many Negroes died trying to gain freedom. Gabriel Prosser headed one try the Negroes made for freedom in 1800 in Virginia.

He was one of those who thought the new day of freedom would dawn only when the slaves themselves went into action. He and his partner, Jack Bowler, were the planners and leaders of a revolt by the slaves in Henrico County, Virginia. They could not get fire-arms, so they collected clubs and swords for months in advance of the day of decision.

On August 30th, 1800, more than a thousand slaves gathered a few miles from Charleston. They started to march on the city. A terrible downpour of rain and strong winds almost broke up the parade of rebels making their strike for freedom.

Two slaves told the whites of this plan, and the Governor of Virginia found out about it. He sent 600 soldiers, and they arrested a large number of slaves. Thirty-five of the slaves were killed. Gabriel Prosser himself was arrested a month later and was put to death. He died without answering any questions that the authorities asked.

The failure of Prosser's try for freedom did not stop the terrible feeling of unrest of the slaves, nor did it stop their plots to free themselves. Because plans had to be kept secret, nobody could really tell how many blacks (and some whites) were taking part in the plots. It was at least 2000; it may have been as many as 50,000. Slaves who were questioned refused to answer even when they knew they would be killed for keeping silent. Many were beaten, branded with hot irons like animals, or hanged. Troops shot them down, or they were put to death after being found guilty after short trials.

Just the same, the plots continued. One of the most complicated ones was made and led by Denmark Vesey. For twenty years after he had bought his freedom with $1,500 he had won in a lottery, Vesey lived in Charleston, South Carolina. He worked as a carpenter, and made a good living. But Denmark's own freedom did not free him from thinking about other blacks who were slaves in bondage. He loved liberty; he wanted equality for all. He made up his mind to help the blacks who were still slaves.

Denmark worked slowly on his plot. He picked his helpers with great care. Their plans took a few years. They collected clubs, bayonets, and daggers. Denmark chose the second Sunday in July, 1822, for the big revolt. However, a slave who had been asked to join in the action told his owner about the plot on May 30th. The whites were ready; 131 blacks and four whites were arrested. All were punished. Thirty-seven Negroes were put to death; the whites paid a fine and went to jail.

Even this did not put a stop to the freedom movement. One of the most famous fights was led by Nat Turner in Virginia in 1831. Although it ended in failure, it became a great historic date in American history as the high point of the slave uprisings.

Nat Turner was a strange man. He ran away from his master, but he returned to him and to slavery even though he was never caught. He was a mystic, a person who believed in "signs" from heaven—signals from God telling him what to do, and when to do it. In his own story he said, "I surely would be a prophet, as the Lord has shown me things that had happened before my birth . . . I was intended for some great purpose, which they (my mother and grandmother) had always thought from certain marks on my head and breast."

One of the signs from heaven that Nat thought was meant for him was the eclipse of the sun which took place in February, 1831. He took this to mean he should lead the Negroes out of slavery. Independence Day, the 4th of July, was the date Nat chose for his revolt. But he got sick and decided that his illness was another sign, a sign to delay the uprising. When he saw the sun turn a peculiar greenish blue on August 13th, the date August 21st came to him as the right time for the revolt.

On the chosen date, Southampton County, Virginia became the scene of a twenty-four hour full-scale war. Nat and his followers killed his owner, Joseph Travis, and his whole family. Sixty whites were killed that day before the soldiers arrived. At least 100 blacks were killed. There were thirteen slaves and three free Negroes arrested at once, tried and hanged on the spot.

76

Turner escaped and hid in a cave, but the barking of a dog showed his hiding place. He was caught on October 30th. He was put to death for his actions, but the last words he put into his own story, written in prison, were, "I am here loaded with chains, and willing to suffer the fate that awaits me."

The Negroes did not stand alone in their wish for freedom. The feelings of many people were changing about slavery. The abolitionist movement was growing, but it put white

A slave auction showing a family which would probably be separated

man against white man. The slaveholders got stricter and tougher in ways they used to keep the Negroes down. The abolitionists worked harder and harder, and they showed results. By the time the Civil War started, there were almost half a million free Negroes, almost ten times as many as there were in 1790.

Where would all this violence lead? Slaves starting revolutions, white men killing white abolitionists, slave markets tearing families apart, Negroes helping whites through inventions and discoveries? It would lead in the end to a great war that almost destroyed the Union of the States.

Chapter VIII

The Civil Rights Struggle Begins

The Civil Rights Struggle Begins

The Negroes in the free North were helping to build the nation. Among this group of northern Negroes there were: a ship-builder, inventors, writers of plays and poetry, a world famous minister, and an equally famous actor. They added to the riches of the country in goods, manufacture, and culture. They began the struggle for civil rights.

Although they were able to become rich, successful, and famous, the northern Negroes did not forget their brothers living in slavery. The Constitution put an end to slavery in 1808 by making it against the law in that year. But with such big money to be made from buying and selling slaves, the traders were willing to break the law. In Virginia and Maryland, slave owners who were making less money from growing tobacco went into the business of "growing" slaves, breeding them like animals. In 1835, one hundred and twenty thousand slaves were sold from Virginia into other states.

In 1836, Texans bought and brought twelve thousand slaves into their State against the law.

The free Negroes could not forget this. Every day they were living with the facts of discrimination: segregation,

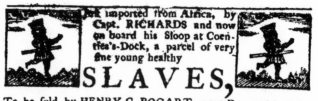

Just imported from Africa, by Capt. RICHARDS and now on board his Sloop at Coentia's-Dock, a parcel of very fine young healthy **SLAVES,**
To be fold by HENRY C. BOGART, next Door to Mr. John Vanderfpiegle.----He has alfo Molaffes for Sale.

NEGROES
FOR SALE.

☞Will be sold at public auction, at Spring Hill, in the County of Hempstead, on a credit of twelve months, on Friday the 28th day of this present month, 15 young and valuable Slaves, consisting of 9 superior Men & Boys, between 12 and 27 years of age, one woman about 43 years who is a good washer and cook, one woman about twenty-seven, and one very likely young woman with three children.
Also at the same time, and on the same terms, three Mules, about forty head of Cattle, plantation tools, one waggon, and a first rate Gin stand, manufactured by Pratt &Co.
Bond with two or more approved securities will be required. Sale to commence at 10 o'clock.
E. E. Hundley,
W. Robinson,
H. M. Robinson.

Two advertisements for slave sales

terrible housing conditions, the worst paying jobs, and the fear of pro-slavery "white supremacy" believers, or whites who were afraid blacks would steal their jobs.

The northern states started putting an end to slavery by the 1830's and completely by the 1840's. Negroes were making progress in business and invention and other activities in spite of the opposition of some whites. Paul Cuffe became a rich owner of land and a builder of ships. He helped thirty-eight Negroes return to Africa by paying their travel expenses. This took place in 1815, showing how early it was thought that one way to solve the problem of slavery was to send the blacks back to Africa.

The first Negro newspaper to appear in America came out in New York City in 1827. It was named *Freedom's Journal*. The name tells you its aim: abolition. It was followed by

FREEDOM'S JOURNAL.

"RIGHTEOUSNESS EXALTETH A NATION."

CORNISH & RUSSWURM,
Editors & Proprietors

NEW-YORK, FRIDAY, MARCH 23, 1827.

[VOL. I. No. 2.

The front page of an issue of *Freedom's Journal*

other Negro-owned and Negro-managed newspapers at the rate of almost one a year for the next thirty years. Some were issued only a few times; most had money troubles, but they all aimed high: equality and freedom for Negroes. The words in their names tell the purpose of these papers: *Mirror of Liberty, The Rights of All, The Impartial Citizen.*

A Philadelphia Negro invented a device to control sails on ships. He had fifty whites and Negroes at work in a factory which made him very rich. This man was James Forten who enlisted before he was fifteen years old as a powder boy—one who carries powder to the guns—on a privateer or privately owned warship. Nobody asked Negroes who joined the Navy any questions as to whether they were runaway slaves, and the ships became good hideouts. The ship James was on was the *Royal Louis,* which was captured, and James spent seven terrible months on the prison ship *Jersey.* As a sailmaker and inventor, after the Revolution, James's wealth amounted to $100,000. He devoted his time and money to the cause of abolition.

A large lumber business in Pennsylvania was owned by a very intelligent and thoughtful Negro, William Whipper. He should be given credit for the idea of changing unfair laws without shooting or looting, called "Non-violent Resistance." It was this idea which made possible Mahatma Gandhi's success in freeing India from English rule, and which was the method preached and practiced later by Dr. Martin Luther King, Jr. in his fight for civil rights.

Whipper was a leader and a spokesman. He expressed himself in words and actions. He started his public appeal for non-violent resistance in 1837 talking before groups at Negro reading societies.

In 1841, the first history of the Negro in America was published. The book was written by a Negro who had been a blacksmith while a slave, and who escaped to the North. This man was James W. C. Pennington. He learned to read and write English. He went to school in Europe where he was taught the classical languages, Latin and Greek, plus French and German. He went to a German University at

Heidelberg, and was graduated with the degree of Doctor of Divinity. He was a minister, like Dr. King, and had a church

The Reverend J. W. C. Pennington, Negro historian

in New York. One of his first demonstrations in 1853 was against street-car segregation to allow Negroes to sit with whites. He was also chairman of a convention of 140 ministers from eight states at Rochester, New York. These men of God expressed high hopes and ideals for Negroes. They were against sending black people back to Africa, and were in favor of education—especially vocational education—better jobs, for Negroes. It was an impressive start, but not much was done after the delegates went home.

In the middle of the nineteenth century, whaling was still a big business. Whale oil was needed very badly. Harpooning the whale was a difficult and dangerous activity. It was a Negro who solved the problem with his invention of the toggle-harpoon. This inventor was a Massachusetts Negro named Lewis Temple.

William Wells Brown

In 1853 William Wells Brown, an escaped slave, had a long story published in book form. It was the first one written by a Negro to appear in print, and was called, "Clotel, or The President's Daughter." It was about the hard life of a part-black family. Brown's writing career continued until 1880 when his last book came out. It was about life in the South, and he called it, "My Southern Home."

In the meantime, Brown added another "first" to American history. He was the author of the first play to be written by a black man and an escaped slave. It came out in 1858, and was called, "The Escape, or A Leap to Freedom."

Brown spent five years in parts of England speaking against slavery before large crowds. He also wrote a travel book, "Three Years in Europe." He stood not only for freedom for the slaves, but also wanted to make other changes in the world that would make it a better place to live in. His other aims were votes for women, better prison conditions, and the establishment of peace in the world.

Perhaps the most popular poet and story teller of the Negro writers was Frances Ellen Watkins Harper. She was born in Maryland of free parents. Frances lost her mother

Frances Ellen Watkins Harper

and father when she was very young. Her uncle, William Watkins, a minister, taught her in his free school for Negroes until she was thirteen years old. She then went to work as a nursemaid in Baltimore. She read a lot, and soon she started to write poems. Some of her poems were printed in newspapers, others in a book.

Living in a free state was what Frances wanted, and so she moved to Ohio. There she taught at Union Seminary at Columbus. Then Frances moved to Pennsylvania to live and teach, and there she worked for the freedom movement. She wrote and spoke for abolition and became one of the most important speakers for the Maine Anti-Slavery Society which paid her a salary as lecturer.

After the Emancipation, she continued to lecture and explain the new way of life for Negroes—the new freedom.

The theatre in the United States gave Negroes a bigger welcome than they received from most other groups. Fame came to many black actors. The most famous was Ira Aldridge. His story starts in 1821 in the section of New York City now known as Greenwich Village. At the corner of Bleecker and Mercer Streets, a mile north of City Hall, there was a theatre where great English plays were acted by the African Company of Negroes. Here Ira Aldridge saw the star, James Hewlett, as Othello and as Richard the Third, plays written by William Shakespeare. Ira was inspired to become an actor, too.

This theatre was in the center of New York's best Negro activities. It was only a short distance from Fraunces Tavern which is still open today as a public restaurant. The Tavern had been owned by Samuel Fraunces, a West Indian Negro, in the time of George Washington. In 1783 Washington

Ira Aldridge, world renowned actor

was the guest of honor of Governor Clinton of New York at a dinner given in the Tavern. It was there he made his famous speech, "A Farewell to His Soldiers."

The African Free School was also in the neighborhood. This school was opened in 1787 by private citizens. Later the City of New York gave money to help support it so that colored children could have a free education. This was a most unusual action since there were no free schools for white children.

Ira Aldridge went to the African Free School. Later he went to the University of Glasgow in Scotland. At this college he met many students who later became anti-slavery leaders; they were the sons of American Negroes who could afford to go to a foreign college where there was no bar to their admission. Ira got high marks in all his subjects, but his real love was acting. Soon he left for London, and not long after was playing the part of Othello at the Royalty Theatre. The part was a "natural" as Othello is a dark-skinned Moor in the play.

Ira acted in other theatres in London, and on the road in England and Europe. He co-starred with Edmund Keane, the greatest English actor of the times. Aldridge became a great friend of the French writer, Alexandre Dumas, author of "The Three Musketeers," who was part Negro himself. The title of Chevalier was given to Ira by the King of Prussia. He performed in the capitol of Sweden by invitation of the King, and also in St. Petersburg (now Leningrad) in Russia.

Meanwhile the African Company in New York closed their theatre because "white hoodlums filled the empty seats and raised such a riot," as recorded by Edith Isaacs, theatrical historian. It was probably this event that kept Aldridge from acting in America, but his influence was still a great force on Negro and white performers in this country because of his known style, voice, graceful ways, and the fame that came to him in the land of his birth which had never seen him act.

JAMES BLAND AND THE MINSTREL MEN

In the plantations of the deep South, slaves entertained themselves, each other, their masters, and their masters' visitors by singing, dancing, and joking. The Negroes had rhythm, originality, and a sense of fun. For holidays or celebrations they practiced, rehearsed, dressed, made up dances and jokes, and put on a whole show. They called it a minstrel show, and the cast was made up of minstrelmen, who were singers of songs of the people. The name minstrel goes back to the times before writing was invented, when these wanderers and travelers told what happened in song.

The plantation minstrel shows were very popular. Often the Negroes who took part in them went around to other plantations to do their act, or even to public places. There is a painting of a minstrel show in Williamsburg, Virginia, in Ludwell-Paradise House. It was painted about 14 years after the Revolution, and is called "The Old Plantation." It shows a banjo and drum being played, as well as a pair of bones, while dancing and singing go on. The bones are real sheep bones which were clicked together like Spanish castanets, to keep time. The player got the name "Mr. Bones," and was later made an important part of regular minstrel shows put together by white actors.

The minstrel shows that white actors arranged were copies of the ones the Negroes first put on. The songs, jokes and dances were taken over by white "minstrel men" who appeared in blackface, put on with burnt cork or black greasepaint make-up.

After the Civil War, Negroes were able to do their own minstrel shows, and earn money for an idea they created.

The greatest names among the minstrels were: Billy Kersands, the dancer; the Bohee Brothers, singers and soft-shoe dancers; and James Bland, master minstrel who wrote and sang "sweet songs." James Bland was born on Long Island, New York, of Negro, Indian, and white parentage.

James Bland, minstrel man and composer

He went to Howard University for a short time, but the music in his blood was too strong. With his banjo he ran away and joined Calender's Minstrels. He toured the U. S. with this company. He wrote some of the great songs of this period such as "Carry Me Back to Ole Virginny," "In the Morning by the Bright Light," and "In the Evening by the Moonlight." Very soon the whole country was singing these great tunes —indeed, they are often sung today.

There were many things wrong with minstrel shows, but some good came out of them. The minstrel shows as performed on the stage by whites before the Civil War, and by blacks after it, made fun of Negroes. This gave a false impression of Negroes which lasted for 150 years. The best part of the shows was the chance given Negroes to develop their talents as musicians, song writers, singers, actors, and dancers. The minstrel show opened the door of the theatre to Negroes, and made them welcome once inside. It gave them the democratic chance to produce the Sidney Poitiers and Bill Cosbys of today, and the opportunity to gain respect, fame, and wealth.

Frederick Douglass was a runaway slave. He wrote the story of his life as a slave in an autobiography which he called "Narrative of the Life of Frederick Douglass." It was first published in book form in 1845. It tells of his fight against slavery and his struggle to make the whole world a better place for everyone. Most freed Negroes wanted more than just abolition; they had great ideas for making the world a good place to live in. Douglass was one of them. He was so highly thought of that he became an adviser to President Lincoln.

Douglass was a great speaker. He was chairman of the Committee on Declaration at the Convention of Ministers in Rochester in 1853. What he "declared" there was that Negroes born in the United States should not be treated as strangers.

Douglass was also a great writer for the cause of freedom. He put out a weekly paper called *The North Star*. All who read it saw the sadness and unfairness of slavery.

Many honors came to Frederick Douglass. When the 15th Amendment was added to the Constitution, guaranteeing that neither race nor color could prevent a person from voting, it was this ex-slave who hailed it. How right that a runaway was chosen to speak! And he said, in honor of this celebration, "Everything is possible to us." Other honors came. He was

Frederick Douglass at his desk in his Washington office

made Marshal of the District of Columbia. This is where the nation's Capitol, Washington, is located, and it was there that the first Negro unions started. Douglass also had a leading part in organization work. He was a noble member of his race, and he ennobled the land where he once was a slave.

John Mercer Langston, great abolitionist leader

John Mercer Langston broke the political ice by being the first Negro ever to get elected to office in the United States. He also became American minister to the island country of Haiti.

Today, by law, no school may be segregated, that is, have students of all one color, or mostly one color. The Supreme

Court decision of 1954 that made this a constitutional law and ordered that all schools integrate was a great victory for the Negroes. The first battle to integrate schools started in 1849 and ended in 1855. A little colored girl, six years old, living in Boston, had to go to a Negro school. On her way to school she passed five white schools, all nearer her home, and also of better quality.

A famous lawyer took the case to court. He lost the case, and little Sarah Roberts was not allowed into a white school, but he won a victory just the same. There began much protest against all-white and all-Negro schools. In 1855 the law-makers ordered that this segregation should be ended. It took another 100 years until the Supreme Court enforced this decision, in another case which made it national law, and it was a long and bitter battle. It took a long time for the 1808 deadline on the slave trade to come to an end. It is taking a long time for the 1954 Supreme Court decision ending segregated schools to be carried out in real life. The battle for equal rights and justice is not yet over.

Chapter IX

The Land Divided

The Land Divided

The slave question became the most important issue, or debate, in the United States. Our nation became a land divided by people for and against slavery. The slaves themselves were a cause and a part of the terrible and violent disagreement over slavery. No Negro was neutral. The freed slaves helped those who were still owned by their masters.

Progress was being made in the abolition movement before the Civil War. The North passed laws to end slavery by the 1830's. There was a revolution by the slaves going on, and they were being helped by the abolitionists.

While this revolt got its start in 1829, it was far from being the first strike against slavery in the New World. We forget that the history of slavery goes back to times even before young Captain Antonio Gonsalves brought the first Africans to Portugal in 1441. Tribes that had won battles made slaves of their enemies; blacks were also made slaves by other blacks to punish them for breaking the laws of the tribe. Slavery became a trade only when the whites became the buyers. Even then, it was the chiefs of the tribes who sold their own people. They also raided other tribes to get the slaves to deliver. The white buyer's beads, rum and tobacco were not easy to resist.

But the slaves hated slavery. On ships going to the New World it was difficult keeping order. This was the most dangerous part of the voyage. The Negroes were branded, put in leg irons, and given just enough space to lie down. They rebelled. They refused to eat. They killed themselves by jumping overboard when they could. They put up no natural resistance against sickness and disease. When they arrived in the West Indies, they were worse off than ever, being so badly treated that uprisings against the whites started as early as 1522, in Hispaniola, and they were followed by more in Puerto Rico, Cuba, and the Virgin Islands.

Sugar became less important in these islands, and the slaves were less needed. They were sold to the mainland where cotton plantations needed them. Through almost three hundred years the fight for freedom never died. The year 1829 is called the beginning of the real fight for freedom because on that date a printed "Call to Arms" was issued. It was a pamphlet called *Appeal* written by David Walker, a free Negro; it called upon all slaves to rise up and rebel against their masters.

Two years after *Appeal* came out, a new voice was heard. It was soon to be heard throughout the land. The voice was that of William Lloyd Garrison, a white man, and an abolitionist who was not just against slavery, but who seemed to see the struggle through the eyes of a slave!

William Lloyd Garrison, white abolitionist leader

Conventions of Negro ministers were used as speaking places for abolition. At the second yearly convention of this kind, Garrison made a speech in favor of everything the Negroes wanted. He was then just beginning his career as an active abolitionist, and later would become famous in American history for the part he played.

In 1831 Garrison became the editor of a new paper, *The Liberator,* which was to become the voice of abolition. Two years later, he formed the very active New England Anti-Slavery Society. From 1840 to 1865, a quarter of a century, Garrison was president of the American Anti-Slavery Society

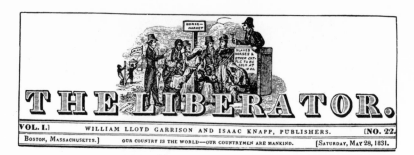

The Liberator's banner, showing a drawing of a market for horses and humans

which was formed after the New England one. Garrison was considered a most powerful enemy by southern slave owners. He seemed to speak like the prophets in the Bible, breathing fire, never giving an inch to his sworn enemies, the slave owners.

David Walker and William Lloyd Garrison are examples of a black and a white having important parts in the abolitionist movement. There were many Negroes and whites, many men and women, who wrote or spoke for the cause, and many who got right into the action of helping slaves escape, and putting them aboard the Underground Railroad—a system of helping slaves escape. They fought police officers and federal marshals to keep them from capturing runaway slaves.

The roll call of Negro and white abolitionists was a long one. The bitterness of the differences between North and South was caused by the fact that the abolitionist fight was going on in the North while the slaves were in the South. The two sections of the country were fighting each other in many ways before the beginning of the Civil War.

Today's riots and violence are a strange echo from the past. But before the Civil War, the violence was against

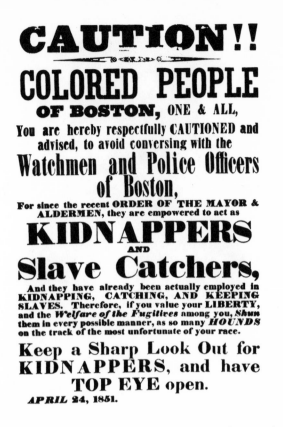

CAUTION!!

COLORED PEOPLE

OF BOSTON, ONE & ALL,

You are hereby respectfully CAUTIONED and advised, to avoid conversing with the

Watchmen and Police Officers of Boston,

For since the recent ORDER OF THE MAYOR & ALDERMEN, they are empowered to act as

KIDNAPPERS

AND

Slave Catchers,

And they have already been actually employed in KIDNAPPING, CATCHING, AND KEEPING SLAVES. Therefore, if you value your LIBERTY, and the *Welfare of the Fugitives* among you, *Shun* them in every possible manner, as so many *HOUNDS* on the track of the most unfortunate of your race.

Keep a Sharp Look Out for KIDNAPPERS, and have TOP EYE open.

APRIL 24, 1851.

Boston advertisement warning slaves to be cautious

the anti-slavery leaders. The pro-slavery forces once tried to murder the anti-slavery leader in Cincinnati, Ohio.

Elijah P. Lovejoy was a white minister who died for his belief that slavery was a sin. He not only preached against it, but also published the abolitionist paper, *The Alton Observer*. A vicious mob shot him to death in Alton, Illinois, August, 1837, and dumped his printing machinery into the river.

The South thought the book *Uncle Tom's Cabin* by Harriet Beecher Stowe almost a crime against nature. One Negro who was caught reading it received a ten year jail sentence.

103

Harriet Beecher Stowe

The book was published in 1851, and was an unexpected, immediate success. It is a highly dramatic story about the love of a child for a slave, of the terrible sufferings of the slaves, and the inhuman ways the slave-drivers treated their victims. It was translated into thirty-six languages, read and cried over throughout the world. It was made into a play, and was acted on the stage all over the world for many years. There is a story told that it played for so many years at the Academy of Music on Fourteenth Street in New York City that real flowers and vegetables were growing on the stage set of the plantation! The whole world seemed to turn against slavery because of this book. The whole world—except the Cotton Kingdom!

While sympathy and tears flowed over the tragedy of

Uncle Tom, active help continued to be given to the slaves by the Underground Railroad. This was a system to get the slaves to the North, run by about 3000 anti-slavery helpers. They moved the slaves on a Saturday to take advantage of the Sundays when their masters could not advertise for the runaways. On the "stations" along the way, the slaves received all the supplies they needed to keep going. They were given clothing and any possible means of transportation: horses, buggies, rowboats. They were lent white babies and were disguised as nurses or mammies. They were paraded as mourners following fake funerals. The Underground even arranged to mail a slave to the North by the Adams Express Company.

The cause of abolition was not limited to the United States. Thinkers in England, Ireland and France who wanted to make a better world spoke and wrote against slavery. Action seemed to be exploding everywhere. In 1846, the Southerners seeking to get more land, touched off a war with Mexico.

In 1850 the Fugitive Slave Law was passed by Congress. This law became hated, fought over, criticized, and abused. It did not allow the fugitive (runaway slave) to speak up for himself or give any kind of proof of his condition. Unlike all other laws, it did not take the fugitive as innocent until proved guilty—just the opposite. It did not apply only to new runaways. It applied to any fugitive, no matter how long ago he had run away, what kind of life he was leading, or where he was living when he was tracked down and caught.

If the Fugitive Slave Law was meant to keep slavery alive and lawful, it seemed to have the opposite effect. It was such a cruel law that people called it the Bloodhound Bill or the Man-Stealing Law. In the South abolitionists were tarred and feathered, beaten on the way to state lines, or lynched by vicious mobs. Northern lawyers used all their wits to keep slave-catchers from taking their victims back to the South. Vigilantes whisked caught slaves out of the hands of the human bloodhounds. The Underground Railroad unlawfully helped more and more slaves to escape from their lawful owners.

Dred Scott

Ammunition was added to the side of the abolitionists in 1857. The Supreme Court's decision in the famous Dred Scott case meant that slavery would be allowed in the territories (new lands, not yet declared states). In the words of this ruling by the Supreme Court, Negroes were not citizens of the United States.

If the abolitionists needed one more shell to fire after the Dred Scott decision, they got it from John Brown in

John Brown

1859. He was a fanatic. Brown led sixteen white and five Negro followers in a raid on the Federal Arsenal at Harper's Ferry in Virginia. His scheme failed. He was caught, tried, and hanged. But his failure did more for abolition than success might have because of the fame he gained as a martyr. He died for a cause he believed in with all his heart, soul, and body. Indeed he became immortal in the song, "John Brown's Body."

The undeclared war between North and South was coming to an end. Soon it would all be out in the open. A new

Abraham Lincoln

party called the Republican Party aimed to keep slavery out
of the West. Slavery divided the Democratic Party; their
strength went with their split. Abraham Lincoln was the
candidate of the new party. He was elected President in
1860. Frightened by the future, the southern states began
to secede from the Union, to declare themselves *not* a part
of the United States. It meant war. Civil War.

Chapter X

The Civil War
1860 - 1865

The Civil War
1860 - 1865

When Abraham Lincoln was sworn in as President of the United States for the second time, in 1865, he said that when the Civil War began one-eighth of the people were slaves. When that war ended, almost four million slaves were freed. Liberty, if not equality, became a fact.

Slavery was the outstanding cause of the Civil War. While there were other causes, the great one was to set enslaved human beings free. Negroes were not only a cause; they played a big part in the war. The stages they played upon were the fields of battle, as cooks and spies behind the front lines, as nurses in hospitals, as workers in relief societies, and as teachers in schools for Negroes. They also worked hard to get the public to stand behind the Union war effort. They worked to put their dream over: to get the right to vote.

The Civil War did not break out openly because of slavery. The states in the South did not feel safe because of the strength of the abolition movement in the North, and because the new Republican Party won the election and Abraham Lincoln was in the White House. The plan of the Southern States was to declare themselves independent of the Union—to secede. They were prepared to fight for this independence. Their first act was to take over Fort Sumter, a federal fort, in Charleston, on the 15th of April, 1861.

Lincoln's answer was an appeal for 75,000 men to enlist in the United States Army. His call was answered by both whites and blacks. At a meeting in the Boston Twelfth Baptist

The 3rd United States Colored Troops (Notice their slogan above)

Church, Negroes offered their money and their lives. Negro regiments in New York, Rhode Island, and Pennsylvania offered to fight as well as to pay for their own wages, food, guns, and uniforms. In Ohio and Michigan, thousands of Negroes volunteered. Their offers were turned down.

Some old ideas were still around: that the black man couldn't become a good soldier, that it was dangerous to put a gun in a black man's hands. Besides the war was started to save the Union. And even Lincoln was against turning it into a war against slavery by changing the black man's rights.

But the Negro could not be ignored. The idea of "forgetting about the Negro" was unthinkable. First, Congress got into action in 1861 by confiscating (taking for the Union side) property used to help the South. Of course, slaves were property—something owned. This taking of property became something used in the war. The next year Congress added more new laws: (1) they made it against the law for army chiefs to return runaway slaves to their owners, (2) they abolished slavery in Washington, D. C. This freed about 3,000 slaves in the Capitol in 1862.

In June 1862 Congress did away with slavery in lands that were not yet states. July 17th 1862, Congress freed all rebel-owned slaves who came under federal control, whether they had been used to help the South or not. The same day, Congress also gave the President the power to have Negroes serve the nation by doing any labor or any war service they were able to. If they were slaves, their mothers, wives, and children were also to be freed.

For a time Lincoln thought he could solve the Negro question by (1) buying their freedom over a 30-year period of time, (2) shipping both free and slave Negroes out of the United States. Both schemes failed. The slaves might have a long wait. Another experiment of sending 500 Negroes to settle land in Haiti was a failure, too. They had to be brought back.

The Negroes did not really want to leave the United States. They felt to be sent away would be just a way of using them to quiet the Southerners who were actually traitors to the Union. Besides, many had homes, owned land, and had their own money.

Lincoln was thinking of proclaiming the freedom of the slaves when he had his schemes tested. He figured the

Emancipation Proclamation would go down easier if there were some place to send the freed slaves. It didn't work. The pace of the war was slowing down. The country needed something to stir it up, "a shot in the arm" for the Union.

Lincoln gave the rebel states a chance to stop fighting. This was in September of 1862. January 1, 1863 he signed the Emancipation Proclamation. What it did was free slaves wherever the rebels had not stopped fighting.

That New Year's Day was one of the greatest days in history. It was celebrated far and wide. The Proclamation itself took its place as a great historical document (important paper) for liberty, next to the Magna Carta and the Declaration of Independence.

While the Emancipation Proclamation was the answer to the dream of millions of Negroes, it was not the final solution to the War or to slavery. It was only a Presidential Proclamation, and did not tell how to put it into action. Second, it applied only to places where the rebellion was still going on. This does not take away from its greatness, but it had a purpose to serve in the War, too. Lincoln knew that by striking at slavery, he would be weakening the fighting power of the South.

The South had to depend heavily on slave workers in their war efforts. Slaves were making gun powder, guns, shoes, saddles, harnesses, wagons, wheels; they were building camps and armories—warehouses where guns and ammunition were kept. They were raising cattle and growing corn, peanuts, and potatoes. It was actually this slave labor that made it possible for the rebels to hold out for four years against the North.

The Emancipation Proclamation made legal what the slaves were already doing in the rebel states. Slaves ran away. When the northern armies came, Negroes joined them. Negroes could now join the army and navy. And they did. There were about 180,000 Negroes who were part of the Union Army, and over one-third of them lost their lives.

The Negro enlisted man was a fine soldier. He went into the service knowing what he was fighting for: to gain self-respect, the respect of others, and a new chance for his sons and daughters. The Negro soldiers fought nobly, even though their training and supplies were not as good at those the whites received. They fought for half-pay for a year and a half. Some northern Negro regiments simply refused to accept the half-pay, and they willingly fought without being paid until this was changed by Congress.

There were about 20,000 Negroes in the Union navy which had always accepted their services if they were free men. After September, 1861, the navy also allowed those who had been slaves to enlist. They received good treatment, lived and ate with white men, and eventually became officers. Many were great heroes. A slave, Robert Smalls, and his Negro crew captured a confederate gunboat in the harbor of Charleston and turned it over to the Union navy. A gunloader on the warship *Kearsage,* Joachim Pease, won the highest praise for his heroism when his ship battled the Confederate ship *Alabama.*

Civilians helped the Union cause, too. Negro women were nurses and cooks in army hospitals and camps. They raised money to buy little extras for soldiers in hospitals, as well as for ex-slaves in the South. They served, they taught, they cheered up the troops and needy slaves who had been freed.

Male civilians were fighting for their rights as citizens, especially for the right to vote. This kind of battle is fought by

A Negro Regiment under attack

getting the public—all the people—behind you. They sent petitions (written requests) to people holding big political jobs, mayors, governors, the President of the United States. They held conventions. One of these drew delegates from eighteen states. It was held in Syracuse, New York, in 1864. The 144 delegates who attended wrote a demand for full manhood rights, including the right to vote. They called their conclusions "Address to the People of the United States."

The "Address" was answered by the passing of the Thirteenth Amendment. This covered the cases of slavery not mentioned or included in the Emancipation Proclamation: *it guaranteed universal freedom.* Its passage January 1, 1865 was a most important achievement.

Four months later, more history was made.

On April 9, 1865, General Robert E. Lee surrendered to General Ulysses S. Grant. The Civil War was over. The North had won. The Union would stand.

April 14, 1865, John Wilkes Booth, an actor playing at Ford's Theatre in Washington, D. C., shot Abraham Lincoln as he was watching the play from a box in the theatre. Lincoln died the next day, and there can be no doubt that this beloved man was mourned by the Negroes of the whole country. He was their great friend. He gave them a feeling of being an important part of America, of belonging to our great nation.

Thus it was that on two days of April, 1865, two great events took place in the history of the American Negro. Each had exactly the opposite effect of the other. Lee's surrender leading to the downfall of the Confederacy was cause to celebrate. The assassination of Lincoln was cause for mourning.

Still the Negroes felt hopeful. They felt that with the end of slavery a new day was dawning for them. They were proud of the help they had given to the nation. They felt it gave them a real share in America's history. They felt this land was now their own.

THE DECLARATION OF INDEPENDENCE

In CONGRESS, July 4, 1776

THE UNANIMOUS DECLARATION of the thirteen united STATES OF
AMERICA.

WHEN in the Course of human events it becomes necessary for one people to dissolve the political bands which have connected them with another, and to assume among the powers of the earth, the separate and equal station to which the Laws of Nature and of Nature's God entitle them, a decent respect to the opinions of mankind requires that they should declare the causes which impel them to the separation.

We hold these truths to be self-evident, that all men are created equal, that they are endowed by their Creator with certain unalienable Rights, that among these are Life, Liberty and the pursuit of Happiness.—That to secure these rights, Governments are instituted among Men, deriving their just powers from the consent of the governed,—That whenever any Form of Government becomes destructive of these ends, it is the Right of the People to alter or to abolish it, and to institute new Government, laying its foundation on such principles and organizing its powers in such form, as to them shall seem most likely to effect their Safety and Happiness. Prudence, indeed, will dictate that Governments long established should not be changed for light and transient causes; and accordingly all experience hath shewn that mankind are more disposed to suffer, while evils are sufferable, than to right themselves by abolishing the forms to which they are accustomed. But when a long train of abuses and usurpations, pursuing invariably the same Object evinces a design to reduce them under absolute Despotism, it is their right, it is their duty, to throw off such Government, and to provide new Guards for their future security.—Such has been the patient sufferance of these Colonies; and such is now the necessity which constrains them to alter their former Systems of Government. The history of the present King of Great Britain is a history of repeated injuries and usurpations, all having in direct object the establishment of an absolute Tyranny over these States. To prove this, let Facts be submitted to a candid world.

He has refused his Assent to Laws, the most wholesome and necessary for the public good.

He has forbidden his Governors to pass Laws of immediate and pressing importance, unless suspended in their operation till his Assent should be obtained; and when so suspended, he has utterly neglected to attend to them.

He has refused to pass other Laws for the accommodation of large districts of people, unless those people would relinquish the right of Representation in the Legislature, a right inestimable to them and formidable to tyrants only.

He has called together legislative bodies at places unusual, uncomfortable, and distant from the depository of their Public Records, for the sole purpose of fatiguing them into compliance with his measures.

He has dissolved Representative Houses repeatedly, for opposing with manly firmness his invasions on the rights of the people.

He has refused for a long time, after such dissolutions, to cause others to be elected; whereby the Legislative Powers, incapable of Annihilation, have returned to the People at large for their exercise; the State remaining in the mean time exposed to all the dangers of invasion from without, and convulsions within.

He has endeavoured to prevent the population of these States; for that purpose obstructing the Laws for Naturalization of Foreigners; refusing to pass others to encourage their migrations hither, and raising the conditions of new Appropriations of Lands.

He has obstructed the Administration of Justice, by refusing his Assent to Laws for establishing Judiciary Powers.

He has made Judges dependent on his Will alone, for the tenure of their offices, and the amount and payment of their salaries.

He has erected a multitude of New Offices, and sent hither swarms of Officers to harass our people, and eat out their substance.

He has kept among us, in times of peace, Standing Armies without the Consent of our legislatures.

He has affected to render the Military independent of and superior to the Civil Power.

He has combined with others to subject us to a jurisdiction foreign to our constitution, and unacknowledged by our laws; giving his Assent to their Acts of pretended Legislation:

For quartering large bodies of armed troops among us:

For protecting them, by a mock Trial, from punishment for any Murders which they should commit on the Inhabitants of these States:

For cutting off our Trade with all parts of the world:

For imposing Taxes on us without our Consent:

For depriving us in many cases, of the benefits of Trial by Jury:

For transporting us beyond Seas to be tried for pretended offences:

For abolishing the free System of English Laws in a neighbouring Province, establishing therein an Arbitrary government, and enlarging its Boundaries so as to render it at once an example and fit instrument for introducing the same absolute rule into these Colonies:

For taking away our Charters, abolishing our most valuable Laws and altering fundamentally the Forms of our Governments:

For suspending our own Legislatures, and declaring themselves invested with power to legislate for us in all cases whatsoever.

He has abdicated Government here, by declaring us out of his Protection and waging War against us.

He has plundered our seas, ravaged our Coasts, burnt our towns, and destroyed the lives of our people.

He is at this time transporting large Armies of foreign Mercenaries to compleat the works of death, desolation and tyranny, already begun with circumstances of Cruelty & Perfidy scarcely paralleled in the most barbarous ages, and totally unworthy the Head of a civilized nation.

He has constrained our fellow Citizens taken Captive on the high Seas to bear Arms against their Country, to become the executioners of their friends and Brethren, or to fall themselves by their Hands.

He has excited domestic insurrections amongst us, and has endeavoured to bring on the inhabitants of our frontiers, the merciless Indian Savages, whose known rule of warfare, is an undistinguished destruction of all ages, sexes and conditions.

In every stage of these Oppressions We have Petitioned for Redress in the most humble terms: Our repeated Petitions have been answered only by repeated injury. A Prince, whose character is thus marked by every act which may define a Tyrant, is unfit to be the ruler of a free people.

Nor have We been wanting in attentions to our Brittish brethren. We have warned them from time to time of attempts by their legislature to extend an unwarrantable jurisdiction over us. We have reminded them of the circumstances of our emigration and settlement here. We have appealed to their native justice and magnanimity, and we have conjured them by the ties of our common kindred to disavow these usurpations, which would inevitably interrupt our connections and correspondence. They too have been deaf to the voice of justice and of consanguinity. We must, therefore, acquiesce in the necessity, which denounces our Separation, and hold them, as we hold the rest of mankind, Enemies in War, in Peace Friends.

WE, THEREFORE, the Representatives of the UNITED STATES OF AMERICA, in General Congress, Assembled, appealing to the Supreme Judge of the world for the rectitude of our intentions, do, in the Name, and by Authority of the good People of these Colonies, solemnly publish and declare, That these United Colonies are, and of Right ought to be FREE AND INDEPENDENT STATES; that they are Absolved from all Allegiance to the British Crown, and that all political connection between them and the State of Great Britain, is and ought to be totally dissolved; and that as Free and Independent States, they have full Power to levy War, conclude Peace, contract Alliances, establish Commerce, and to do all other Acts and Things which Independent States may of right do.—And for the support of this Declaration, with a firm reliance on the protection of Divine Providence, we mutually pledge to each other our Lives, our Fortunes and our sacred Honor.

JOHN HANCOCK.

New Hampshire.
Josiah Bartlett,
Wm. Whipple,
Matthew Thornton.

Rhode Island.
Step. Hopkins,
William Ellery.

Connecticut.
Roger Sherman,
Sam'el Huntington,
Wm. Williams,
Oliver Wolcott.

New York.
Wm. Floyd,
Phil. Livingston,
Frans. Lewis,
Lewis Morris.

New Jersey.
Richd. Stockton,
Jno. Witherspoon,
Fras. Hopkinson,
John Hart,
Abra. Clark.

Pennsylvania.
Robt. Morris,
Benjamin Rush,
Benj. Franklin,
John Morton,
Geo. Clymer,
Jas. Smith,
Geo. Taylor,
James Wilson,
Geo. Ross.

Massachusetts-Bay.
Saml. Adams,
John Adams,
Robt. Treat Paine,
Elbridge Gerry.

Delaware.
Caesar Rodney,
Geo. Read,
Tho. M'Kean.

Maryland.
Samuel Chase,
Wm. Paca,
Thos. Stone,
Charles Carroll of Carrollton.

Virginia.
George Wythe,
Richard Henry Lee,
Th. Jefferson,
Benj. Harrison,
Ths. Nelson, Jr.,
Francis Lightfoot Lee,
Carter Braxton.

North Carolina.
Wm. Hooper,
Joseph Hewes,
John Penn.

South Carolina.
Edward Rutledge,
Thos. Heyward, Junr.,
Thomas Lynch, Junr.,
Arthur Middleton.

Georgia.
Button Gwinnett,
Lyman Hall,
Geo. Walton.

IN CONGRESS
JANUARY, 18, 1777.

Ordered:

That an authenticated copy of the Declaration of Independency, with the names of the Members of Congress subscribing the same, be sent to each of the United States, and that they be desired to have the same put on record.

By order of Congress.

Attest, CHAS. THOMSON, *Secy.* A true copy. JOHN HANCOCK, *Presidt.*

The Emancipation Proclamation
January 1, 1863

By the President of the United States of America:

A Proclamation.

Whereas on the 22d day of September, A.D. 1862, a proclamation was issued by the President of the United States, containing, among other things, the following, to wit:

"That on the 1st day of January, A.D. 1863, all persons held as slaves within any State or designated part of a State the people whereof shall then be in rebellion against the United States shall be then, thenceforward, and forever free; and the executive government of the United States, including the military and naval authority thereof, will recognize and maintain the freedom of such persons and will do no act or acts to repress such persons, or any of them, in any efforts they may make for their actual freedom.

"That the executive will on the 1st day of January aforesaid, by proclamation, designate the States and parts of States, if any, in which the people thereof, respectively, shall then be in rebellion against the United States; and the fact that any State or the people thereof shall on that day be in good faith represented in the Congress of the United States by members chosen thereto at elections wherein a majority of the qualified voters of such States shall have participated shall, in the absence of strong countervailing testimony, be deemed conclusive evidence that such State and the people thereof are not then in rebellion against the United States."

Now, therefore, I, Abraham Lincoln, President of the United States, by virtue of the power in me vested as Commander-in-Chief of the Army and Navy of the United States in time of actual armed rebellion against the authority and government of the United States, and as a fit and necessary war measure for suppressing said rebellion, do, on this 1st day of January, A.D. 1863, and in accordance with my purpose so to do, publicly proclaimed for the full period of one hundred days from the first day above mentioned, order and designate as the States and parts of States wherein the people thereof, respectively, are this day in rebellion against the United States the following, to wit:

Arkansas, Texas, Louisiana (except the parishes of St. Bernard, Plaquemines, Jefferson, St. John, St. Charles, St. James, Ascension, Assumption, Terrebonne, Lafourche, St. Mary, St. Martin, and Orleans, including the city of New Orleans), Mississippi, Alabama, Florida, Georgia, South Carolina, North Carolina, and Virginia (except the forty-eight counties designated as West Virginia, and also the counties of Berkeley, Accomac, Northhampton, Elizabeth City, York, Princess Anne, and Norfolk, including the cities of Norfolk and Portsmouth), and which excepted parts are for the present left precisely as if this proclamation were not issued.

And by virtue of the power and for the purpose aforesaid, I do order and declare that all persons held as slaves within said designated States and parts of States are, and henceforward shall be, free; and that the Executive Government of the United States, including the military and naval authorities thereof, will recognize and maintain the freedom of said persons.

And I hereby enjoin upon the people so declared to be free to abstain from all violence, unless in necessary self-defense; and I recommend to them that, in all cases when allowed, they labor faithfully for reasonable wages.

And I further declare and make known that such persons of suitable condition will be received into the armed service of the United States to garrison forts, positions, stations, and other places, and to man vessels of all sorts in said service.

And upon this act, sincerely believed to be an act of justice, warranted by the Constitution upon military necessity, I invoke the considerate judgment of mankind and the gracious favor of Almighty God.

Index